Modal Verbs

Allaberganova Umida

© Allaberganova Umida
Modal Verbs
By: Allaberganova Umida
Edition: June '2025
Publisher:
Taemeer Publications LLC (Michigan, USA / Hyderabad, India)

© **Allaberganova Umida**

Book	:	**Modal Verbs**
Author/s	:	Allaberganova Umida
Publisher	:	Taemeer Publications
Year	:	'2025
Pages	:	76
Title Design	:	*Taemeer Web Design*

Learning requires not only grammatical knowledge, but also the ability to express thoughts correctly and clearly in communication. In this regard, modal verbs in English (can, could, must, have to, may, might, need, should, shall, will, would) occupy a special place as important grammatical units. Through them, the student can express meanings such as probability, obligation, permission, opportunity and necessity.

This methodological manual is dedicated to the topic "Modal Verbs", in which language learners will get acquainted with the meaning, use and differences of modal verbs. The manual also contains many examples of the correct use of modal verbs, interactive exercises, creative tasks and dialogues related to real-life situations.

This guide is designed for teachers, students, and independent learners to help them develop fluency and correct English speaking skills through in-depth mastery of modal verbs. Learn modal verbs — they will give you freedom and clarity in expressing your thoughts!

Understanding Modal Verbs: Should & Would

Page 1: Introduction to Modal Verbs "Should" and "Would"

Modal verbs are helping verbs that convey meanings like obligation, likelihood, permission, or capability. Among them, "should" and "would" are frequently used to give suggestions, discuss imagined scenarios, or make courteous requests.

1. Should

Usage: To offer suggestions, indicate what is likely, or describe a responsibility.

Explanation:
We commonly use "should" to recommend the proper course of action or to express what we believe will occur.

Examples:
It's a good idea to review your notes before the test. (Advice)
He's probably at home already. (Expectation)
It's important for drivers to follow the rules of the road. (Duty)

2. Would

Usage: To describe imagined scenarios, make

courteous requests, or refer to repeated actions in the past.

Explanation:

Although "would" is technically the past form of "will," it is mainly used in polite expressions or to talk about unreal or imagined situations.

Examples:

If I had the money, I'd explore different countries. (Imagined situation)

Would you care for some coffee? (Polite request)

As a kid, we used to go to my grandparents' house every summer. (Past routine)

Comparing "Should" and "Would"

Modal Verb

Primary Functions

Illustrative Sentences

Should

Used for giving recommendations, expressing what is expected, or describing responsibilities.

You ought to work out regularly.

She is likely to get here by midday.

Would

Used in imagined situations, to ask politely, or describe past routines.

If it were possible, I'd purchase a car.

Could you lend me a hand?
We used to go hiking every weekend.
Extra Examples:
Do you think we should head out now or wait?
If I were in your position, I'd accept the offer.
It might be best to consult a doctor.
Would it be okay if you shut the window?

1. Detailed Explanation of 'Should' and 'Would'

1.1 'Should' – Definition, Usage & Examples

The modal verb 'should' is commonly used to offer suggestions, indicate moral duties, express what is expected, or give recommendations. It reflects what is considered appropriate or anticipated in a given context.

Functions of 'Should':

Offering Advice:
You ought to get more rest.
She needs to prepare better for the test.

Stating Obligations:
Everyone ought to treat others with respect.
It's important to wear a seatbelt.

Recommending Something:
You might want to check out the new restaurant.

Indicating Expectations:
The train is expected to arrive at 10.
Expressing Regret or Criticism About the Past (Should have + past participle):
You ought to have called me sooner.
Structure:
Affirmative Form:
Structure: Subject + should + base verb
Example: You should pay attention.
Negative Form:
Structure: Subject + shouldn't + base verb
Example: You shouldn't miss breakfast.
Question Form:
Structure: Should + subject + base verb?
Example: Should we bring a present?

1.2 'Would' – Definition, Usage & Examples

The modal verb 'would' is used to talk about imagined or unreal situations, make polite suggestions or offers, express personal preferences, describe routines from the past, and refer to events that were expected to happen in the past.

- Hypothetical Situations:
If I had a lot of money, I'd explore different countries around the globe.
- Polite Requests/Offers:

Would you care for some coffee?
Would it be alright if you opened the window?
- Expressing Preferences:
I would prefer to stay home.
She would rather have tea than coffee.
- Past Habits:
When we were children, we would spend all day playing outside.
- Future in the Past:
He mentioned that he would get in touch with me later.

Structure:
Positive form: Subject + would + base form of the verb (e.g., I would assist you.)
Negative form: Subject + wouldn't + base form of the verb (e.g., She wouldn't attend.)
Interrogative form: Would + subject + base form of the verb? (e.g., Would you join us?)

Page 3: Exercise

Exercise 1: Fill in the blanks Fill in each blank with either should or would.
1. You __ consult a doctor about that cough.
2. If I had more time, I __ take up Spanish.
3. He __ ever be dishonest with his friends.
4. __ you give me a hand with this bag?
5. We __ go hiking every weekend when we

lived in Switzerland.
Exercise 2: Correct or Incorrect? Mark each sentence as Correct or Incorrect.
1. You should to complete your homework before you start playing.
2. I would phone you if I had your number.
3. He should goes to the gym on a regular basis.
4. Would you mind opening the window?
5. She should arrive at work by 9 in the morning.
Exercise 3: Rewrite the following sentences using "should" or "would"
1. Eating nutritious food is recommended. → _____
2. I'm wondering if you are able to assist me. → _____
3. He used to play chess with his dad regularly in the past. → _____
Exercise 4: Fill in the blanks with "should" or "would"
Exercise 3: Rewrite the following sentences using "should" or "would"
1. Eating nutritious food is recommended. → _____
2. I'm wondering if you are able to assist me.

→ _____

3. He used to play chess with his dad regularly in the past. → _____

Exercise 5: Rewrite the sentences using "should" or "would"

1. Drinking water is recommended. → You ____ drink water.
2. He is kind and willing to assist. → He ____ always help others.

Exercise 6: Choose the correct modal verb

1. If I had more free time, I (should/would) start learning a new language.
2. You (should/would) put on a jacket—it's chilly out there.

Exercise 7: Correct the mistakes

1. He would eats vegetables every day. → ____
2. Should you mind helping me? → ____

Exercise 8: Translate into English using "should" or "would"

1. Men har kuni kitob o'qishim kerak. → _____

2. Agar imkonim bo'lsa, men yangi uy olgan bo'lardim. → _____

Vocabulary (20 Words)
1.   Advice

2. Expectation
3. Duty
4. Hypothetical
5. Polite
6. Request
7. Situation
8. Habitual
9. Possibility
10. Necessity
11. Offer
12. Suggestion
13. Recommendation
14. Future
15. Past
16. Action
17. Condition
18. Result
19. Respectfully
20. Etiquette

Activities & Games
Group Activity:
- In pairs, students create dialogues using "should" and "would" in different contexts (advice, requests, past habits).
Activity

Role Play:
Work in pairs. Student A is a doctor, Student B is a patient. Use "should" to give and receive advice about health. Then switch roles.

Example:
B: I have a headache and can't sleep well.
A: You should drink less coffee and go to bed earlier.

Picture Game:
- Show a picture of various scenarios (e.g., a sick person, a messy room, a lost wallet).
- Ask: "What should he/she do?" or "What would you do in this situation?"

Activity Title: Advice Booth & Imagination Time!

Grammar Focus: "Would" (hypothetical situations), "Should" (giving advice)

Age/Level: A2–B1

Group Size: Pairs or Small Groups

Time: 30–40 minutes

 Part 1: The Advice Booth (for "Should")

Objective: Practice giving advice using "should."

How to Play:
1. Prepare slips of paper with common teen dilemmas, such as:

"I forgot my homework again."
"My best friend is mad at me."
"I want to get a pet, but my parents said no."
"I play video games all night and feel tired at school."
2. One student picks a card and reads the problem aloud. The others become "advice-givers" in the Advice Booth.
3. They must respond using "should":
"You should talk to your teacher."
"You shouldn't stay up so late."
4. Vote for the best advice (optional).
 Variation: Make it dramatic! Students act out the dilemma and advice.
 Part 2: What Would You Do? (for "Would")
Objective: Practice hypothetical thinking using "would."
How to Play:
1. Use or create "What would you do if...?" questions:
"What would you do if you found a wallet full of money?"
"What would you do if you could fly?"
"What would you do if you were invisible for a day?"

2. Students work in pairs or groups to discuss their answers using "would":
"I would keep it safe and try to find the owner."
"I would fly to school every day!"
3. Share answers with the class — the most creative answer wins a small prize or point.
Variation: Turn it into a story chain. One student starts: "If I could fly, I would go to Paris." Next student adds a sentence with "would," building a fun hypothetical story.

Learning Outcome:
Students differentiate between giving advice (should) and imagining hypotheticals (would).
They speak and listen actively in a fun, low-pressure environment.

Reading Activity
Read the following paragraph and identify the use of 'should' and 'would'.

Last summer, my family and I went on a trip to the mountains. Each morning, we would take long walks through the trails, and in the evenings, we would gather around the campfire to share stories. The entire experience was truly memorable. I believe that more families should make time to bond in this way. It's important for people to step away from their busy routines and connect with nature to refresh themselves. If I had the chance, I would spend every weekend like that. Wouldn't you enjoy unwinding in such a calm and quiet place?

Comprehension Questions

1. How was the speaker's summer experience?
2. What activities did they do every morning and evening?
3. How many times are 'should' and 'would' used in the passage?
4. What advice does the speaker give?
5. What hypothetical situation is described?

Questions about the topic:
With "Should":
1. Should people exercise every day to stay healthy?
2. What should you do if you see someone in need of help?
3. Should students be allowed to use phones in

class?
4. Where should we go for our next vacation?
5. Should you always follow your parents' advice?
With "Would":
6. What would you do if you won a million dollars?
7. Would you move to another country for your dream job?
8. If you had the chance, would you learn another language?
9. Would you prefer tea or coffee in the morning?
10. When you were younger, what games would you play with your friends?

Writing Task

Write a short paragraph (100-150 words) about a time you gave or received advice using "should," or about an imaginary situation using "would."

Glossary

Advice – a suggestion about what someone should do

Expectation – a belief that something will happen

Hypothetical – imagined or possible, not real

Polite – showing good manners
Request – the act of asking for something
Habitual – done regularly
Offer – to present something for someone to accept
Suggestion – an idea or plan offered for consideration
Duty – something that one is expected or required to do
Etiquette – polite behavior in society

MODAL VERBS: CAN, MUST AND HAVE TO

"Can" is a modal verb used to indicate ability, possibility, permission, or to make a request. It shows that the subject has the capability to perform an action. In contrast, the negative forms "cannot" or "can't" are used to show that the subject is not able to do something.

Structure:

The sentence pattern is: Subject + can + base verb

Examples:
- I can swim.
- She can speak English.

Uses of "Can"

a) Ability – To show that someone knows how to do something or has the skill

Examples:
- He knows how to play the guitar.
- They are able to solve this issue.

b) Permission – To give or request the right to do something

Examples:
- You are allowed to leave now.

• May I use your phone?

c) Possibility – To express that something might happen or be true

Examples:

• Winters can be extremely cold.

• Issues can arise at any moment.

d) Request – To politely ask someone to do something

Examples:

• Could you please assist me?

• May I ask a question?

Negative Form: "Can't" or "Cannot"

Used when the subject is not able to do something

Examples:

• I am not able to swim.

• She is unable to drive a car.

Question Form:

The structure is: Can + subject + base verb?

Examples:

• Are you able to play the piano?

• Is he allowed to come with us?

Short Answers:

• Yes, I can. / No, I can't.

A. Complete the Sentences Using "Can" or "Can't"

1. I ___ know how to ride a bicycle.
2. She ___ understand and speak Japanese.
3. They ___ attend the party today.
4. We ___ play soccer after school.
5. He ___ see clearly without his glasses.

B. Choose the Right Option

1. He ___ perform very well on the piano.
a) can
b) can't

2. ___ you assist me with this bag?
a) Can
b) Can't

3. I ___ make sense of this question. It's too confusing.
a) can
b) can't

4. She ___ read books written in English.
a) can
b) can't

5. ___ they visit our house today?
a) Can
b) Can't

C. Finish the Sentences Using "Can" or "Can't" Plus an Appropriate Verb

1. I ___ (carry) this package—it's far too heavy!

2. She ___ (speak) three different languages fluently.
3. We ___ (visit) the museum if we manage to finish our tasks early.
4. They ___ (find) their way without using a map. It's too tricky.
5. You ___ (see) the mountains from the balcony on a clear day.

Role Play Activity: "The Rule Makers" – Creating and Enforcing Rules

Target Grammar: must (for rules, obligations, strong necessity)

Level: A2–B1 (Pre-Intermediate to Intermediate)
Skills Practiced: Speaking, Listening, Grammar
Group Size: Pairs or small groups
 Scenario:
The class is transformed into a team of school officials, camp counselors, or apartment managers who must create a list of rules for a specific place or situation.

Each group chooses or is assigned one of the following settings:

1. A new English language school
2. A summer camp for teenagers
3. A shared student apartment
4. A zoo
5. A space station (for creativity!)
6. A hospital
7. A football team

Instructions:
1. Step 1: Create Rules (10 minutes)

In groups, students brainstorm and write 5–7 rules using must.

Example:

"Students must speak only English in class."
"Campers must stay in their cabins after 10 p.m."
"You must wash your hands before feeding the animals."

2. Step 2: Role Play (10–15 minutes)

One student plays a new member who keeps breaking the rules.

The rest of the group corrects them using must.

Example:

"I don't want to wear my name tag."
"You must wear your name tag at all times!"

3. Step 3: Present or Perform

Each group presents their "rule world" to the class.
Optional: Act out one short rule-breaking scene and correction.

Language Focus:
Reinforces use of must for strong rules and formal obligations.
Encourages polite but firm speech:
"You must not do that here."
"Everyone must arrive on time."
Why it works:
Interactive and student-centered
Realistic + imaginative options
Builds vocabulary around responsibility and daily routines

D. Rewrite the sentences as questions using "can"

1. He plays the guitar very well.
→ _____?
2. She works on weekends.
→ "can" or "can't"
3. They use this program easily.
→ "can" or "can't"
4. We park our car here.
→ "can" or "can't"

5. You help me with this project.
→ "can" or "can't"

E. Choose the correct option

1. My grandmother is 80, but she ___ use a smartphone.
a) can
b) can't

2. ___ you understand this text without a dictionary?
a) Can
b) Can't

3. We ___ finish the report before Friday. The deadline is strict.
a) can't
b) can

4. I'm afraid I ___ come to the meeting today. I'm sick.
a) can
b) can't

5. She ___ solve difficult problems quickly. She's very smart.
a) can
b) can't

. True or false?
Read and circle true or false for these sentences.

I know lots of sports. I can swim and I can play football. I can play basketball too because we practise at school! But I can't play tennis. What else can I do? Well, I can't speak German or French but I can speak English and Arabic!

a. She can swim. true false
b. She can't play football. true false
c. She practises basketball at school. true false
d. She can play tennis. true false
e. She can't speak Arabic. true false

2. Choose the answer!
Read the sentence. Circle the correct answer.
a. I can . to swim / swim / swimming
b. She ride a bike. can / cans / know
c. Can you tennis? plays / to play / play
d. He speak Spanish. isn't / can'ts / can't
e. run fast? They can / Can they / Are they
f. He can't five pizzas! eat / ate / to eat
g. We dinner. can to cook / can cook / can cooking

3. Make it right!
Find the mistake in each sentence and correct it.
a. She can't driving a car. She can't drive a car.

b. I can't to play chess.
c. He cans make a cake.
d. They can't to sing very well.
e. Can you eating with chopsticks?
f. She can't ride a horse.
g. He can speaking three languages.
h. How many musical instruments you can play?
4. Write and draw!
What sports can you play? What languages can you speak? What else can
you do? Write about yourself like in exercise 1 and draw a picture!
Vocabulary
Ability
Possibility
Permission
Request
Solve
Understand
Heavy
Early
Read
Draw
Language
Write

Make
Find
Mistakes
Choose
Because

1. Find correct word
Mopserisn-
Sektaims-
Dinf-
Ngaugale-
Ohcsoe-
Biality-

2. Give a definition
Ability-
Possibility-
Permission -
Request-
Solve-
Understand-
Heavy-
Early-
Language-
Make-
Find-

Mistakes-
Must, Have to and Has to

Must or Have to? Must only has a present form, so we need to use have to for all other verb forms (past, future, perfect forms, infinitive, etc.). You will have to come with me. We had to drive very fast. All three are used to express obligation or necessity, but with small differences in meaning and use:

Must
Strong personal obligation or advice
I must finish this project today.

Have to
General obligation or rules (external)
We have to wear a uniform at work.

Has to
Same as "have to" (3rd person singular)
She has to go to the meeting.

2. Structure
- I/You/We/They → have to + verb
- He/She/It → has to + verb
- All subjects → must + verb

3. Examples
Obligation / Necessity
- I have to study every day.
- He has to wear glasses at school.

- You must listen carefully.
    Rules / Laws
- We have to pay taxes.
- People must stop at red lights.
- She has to follow the school rules.

TESTS:

A. MUST (obligation / strong necessity)

1. You ___ wear a helmet when riding a bike.
(must / can / have to)

2. She ___ be at work by 8 a.m., or she will be late.
(must / can / has to)

3. We ___ forget our passports!
(must / mustn't / can't)

4. ___ I finish the project today?
(Can / Must / Do)

5. Students ___ cheat in exams.
(mustn't / don't have to / can't)

B. HAVE TO (external obligation / rules / routines)

6. I ___ go to school on Saturdays.
(don't have to / must / can't)

7. She ___ study every evening. It's part of her schedule.
(has to / must / can)

8. They ___ bring their own lunch to the

picnic.
(have to / must / has to)
9. Do you ___ do your homework before dinner?
(must / have to / has to)
10. He ___ wear a tie to work, but it's not necessary.
(has to / mustn't / doesn't have to)
C. CAN (ability / permission / possibility)
11. I ___ speak three languages.
(can / must / have to)
12. ___ I borrow your book, please?
(Have to / Must / Can)
13. We ___ go to the park if it doesn't rain.
(can / must / have to)
14. She ___ play the piano very well.
(can / has to / must)
15. You ___ use your phone during the break.
(can / must / have to)

   EXECISES

A. Complete the sentences with: must, have to, has to

 1. I ___ finish this report by tonight. It's urgent.
 2. She ___ get up early tomorrow for a job interview.

3. You ___ wear a helmet when riding a bike. It's the law.
4. We ___ be quiet in the library.
5. They ___ take their son to the doctor today.
6. He ___ study more if he wants to pass the exam.

B. Choose the correct option
1. You must / have to try this dessert – it's delicious!
2. He has to / must go to the dentist at 3 PM.
3. I must / has to remember her birthday.
4. My parents have to / must pay the electricity bill today.
5. She must / have to do her homework now — it's due tomorrow.

C. Rewrite the sentences in the negative form
1. You have to bring your passport.
→
_____
–
2. He has to go to school on Saturday.
→
3. We must answer all the questions.
→
4. They have to work late tonight.

→

5. She must wear a uniform.

→

D. Make questions using: Do/Does ... have to? or Must ...?

1. (she / do her homework)

→

_____

2. (you / wear a uniform at work)

→

3. (they / leave early)

→

4. (he / take the test again)

→

5. (we / bring our ID)

E. Fill in the blanks with affirmative or negative forms of must or have to & has to.

1. It's raining outside. Jim must take his umbrella.

2. I can give you my car, so you ____ buy a new one.

3. They ____ be in a hurry, because they have got more than
enough time.

4. You ____ stop at the red light.

5. Tomorrow is Sunday. You   get up very early.
6. Mrs. Parks can't see very well. She   wear glasses.
7. You   return them. They are too small for you.
8. I am broke, I   borrow some money to buy a car.
9. You   stop smoking. It is very harmful.
10. Mr. Dickson is travelling abroad this summer, so he   get his passport soon.
11. All the students   obey the school rules.
12. It's freezing outside, so we   take a cab and not walk.
13. Students   look at their notes during the test.
14. I have a terrible headache, so I   leave early.
15. Snow has blocked the roads. We   stay here until it's cleared

GLOSSARY

1. Obligation – something you must do
Example: There is an obligation to wear a uniform at school.
2. Necessity – something important that is needed

Example: Water is a necessity for all living things.

3. Permission – being allowed to do something
Example: You need permission to leave early.

4. Prohibition – something that is not allowed
Example: Smoking is a prohibition in this area.

5. Rule – a guideline you must follow
Example: One rule is to turn off your phone in class.

6. Law – an official rule made by a government
Example: It is the law to pay taxes.

7. Optional – not necessary; your choice
Example: Wearing a tie is optional at this event.

8. Urgent – very important and must be done quickly
Example: This report is urgent. Please finish it today.

9. Responsibility – something you are expected to do
Example: Taking care of your homework is your responsibility.

10. Advice – helpful suggestion or recommendation
Example: My teacher gave me advice to study

more.

Modal Verb: Need

The modal verb 'need' can be used in two main ways: as a modal verb and as a main verb. Let's understand both with examples.

1. 'Need' as a Modal Verb

'Need' is used to express necessity or obligation. It is mostly used in negative and question sentences.

In this case, 'need' is followed by the base form of the main verb (without 'to').

Rules:
-Do not use 'do/does/did' with modal 'need'.
-Use 'need not' or 'needn't' for negative sentences.

Examples:
-You need not come early.
-Need I bring my book?
-He need not worry about the test.

2. 'Need' as a Main Verb

'Need' is also used as a regular/main verb. In this case, it follows normal verb rules and is usually followed by 'to + verb'.

Rules:
-Use 'do/does/did' for negatives and questions.
-Add 's' in present simple third person.

Examples:
- I need to finish my homework.
- He needs to call his mom.
- Do you need to talk to me?
- She doesn't need to go today.

3. Comparison

Modal 'need' is more formal and often used in written English. Main verb 'need' is more common in everyday speech.

Modal Verb: Need

The modal verb 'need' can be used in two main ways: as a modal verb and as a main verb. Let's understand both with examples.

1. 'Need' as a Modal Verb

'Need' is used to express necessity or obligation. It is mostly used in negative and question sentences.

In this case, 'need' is followed by the base form of the main verb (without 'to').

Rules:
- Do not use 'do/does/did' with modal 'need'.
- Use 'need not' or 'needn't' for negative sentences.

Examples:

-You need not come early.
-Need I bring my book?
-He need not worry about the test.

2. 'Need' as a Main Verb

'Need' is also used as a regular/main verb. In this case, it follows normal verb rules and is usually followed by 'to + verb'.

Rules:
-Use 'do/does/did' for negatives and questions.
-Add 's' in present simple third person.

Examples:
-I need to finish my homework.
-He needs to call his mom.
-Do you need to talk to me?
-She doesn't need to go today.

3. Comparison

Modal 'need' is more formal and often used in written English. Main verb 'need' is more common in everyday speech.

Here are some interesting facts about the modal verb "need":

"Need" is both a modal and a main verb:

Modal use: "Need you go now?" (like other modals: can, must)Main verb use: "You need to go now."

Modal "need" is more common in British

English:
British English: "Need you speak so loudly?"
American English prefers: "Do you need to speak so loudly?"
"Need" as a modal is usually used in negative or question forms:Negative: "You needn't worry."
Question: "Need I bring anything?"
"Needn't" is the contracted form of "need not":
Example: "You needn't come if you're busy."
It expresses a lack of necessity, like "don't have to."
"Need" (modal) is followed by the base form of a verb without "to":Correct: "Need I study more?"
Incorrect: "Need I to study more?"
It's used to express necessity or obligation in a polite or formal way:Example: "Need we continue this discussion?"
"Need" as a modal is losing popularity in modern English:
People now prefer forms like "don't need to" or "do you need to."Exercise 1: Choose the correct form of 'need'

1. You (need / need to) bring your ID card.
2. (Need / Do) I finish the project today?
3. She (need / needs) to sleep early.
4. They (need not / do not need to) wait.

Exercise 2: Fill in the blanks with 'need' as modal or main verb 1. You __ not worry.
2. He __ to study for the exam.
3. __ she go now?
4. I __ to leave early today.

Exercise 3: Make your own sentences
Use 'need' as a modal and a main verb in different sentences. Write at least 4 sentences.

Fill in the blanks with "need" or "doesn't need"I ____ to go to the store right now.
You ____ to bring your homework tomorrow.
She __ to study because she already knows the lesson.We __ to hurry, we still have plenty of time.
They ____ to worry about the test.
He ____ to clean his room today.

Choose the correct option (need / don't need)I ____ a pencil for the test.

a) need

b) don't need

You ____ to bring your lunch today.

a) need

b) don't need

They ____ any help right now.

a) need

b) don't need

She ____ to wake up early tomorrow.

a) needs

b) doesn't need

Rewrite the sentences with the correct form of "need"I/need/a pencil.

He/not/need/to study for the test.

We/need/to clean the house.

They/not/need/to go to the doctor.

Fill in the gaps with "need" or "don't need" and a verb

You __ to practice more if you want to improve your skills.They __ to buy new clothes, their old ones are fine.

He ____ to be at the meeting tomorrow.

We __ to call him, he's already on his way.She __ to bring her books to class.

Create questions and answer them using "need" or "don't need"(You / bring a dictionary to class?)

(He / study for the exam?)

(We / arrive early?)

(They / work overtime?)
(I / go to the gym today?)
Match the sentences with the correct meanings.I need to finish my homework.
She doesn't need to buy a new phone.
We need to leave early tomorrow.
He doesn't need to bring anything to the meeting.
a) She already has a new phone.
b) We have a lot of time.
c) I have an important task to complete.
d) He has everything prepared for the meeting.
Complete the sentences with the correct form of "need" (affirmative or negative).
You ____ to write the essay if you already know the topic well.
They ____ to hurry, there is plenty of time before the concert starts.
We ____ to call him, he will arrive soon.
She __ to go to the gym every day to stay fit, but she likes to walk instead.He __ to take a taxi; the bus will be faster.
TESTS:
1. You ___ need to bring your own lunch. Food will be provided.
(a) don't

(b) didn't
(c) needn't
(d) can't

2. ___ I need to complete this assignment today?
(a) Must
(b) Do
(c) Can
(d) Should

3. She ___ need to wear a uniform at her new job.
(a) doesn't
(b) don't
(c) isn't
(d) hasn't

4. You ___ talk to the manager unless it's urgent.
(a) needn't
(b) must
(c) should
(d) can't

5. He ___ need any help. He already finished the work.
(a) didn't
(b) doesn't
(c) hadn't

(d) won't
6. I ___ need to take the test again if I pass this time.
(a) don't
(b) needn't
(c) can't
(d) mustn't
7. They ___ need to submit the form by Friday.
(a) does
(b) do
(c) need
(d) have
8. You ___ need to come if you're busy.
(a) mustn't
(b) can't
(c) don't
(d) needn't
9. What do I ___ to bring for the camping trip?
(a) must
(b) need
(c) should
(d) have
10. Need she finish the report today?
(a) Yes, she must.
(b) Yes, she need.
(c) Yes, she does.

(d) Yes, she needs.

Choose the correct sentence.a) I need to explain this to her.

b) I needs to explain this to her.

c) I need explaining this to her.

a) She need to study for the test.

b) She needs to study for the test.c) She need studying for the test.

a) They need not worrying about it.b) They need not to worry about it.c) They need not worry about it.

Write a short dialogue using "need" (5-7 sentences).Example:

A: Do you need help with your homework?

B: No, I don't need help. I think I understand it now.

A: Are you sure?

B: Yes, but I need to focus more on the math problems.A: Okay, just let me know if you need anything.

Games for Learning 'Need'

Game 1: Need It or Not?

Materials: Flashcards with actions (e.g., 'bring an umbrella', 'do homework', etc.)How to Play:

1. Divide the class into two teams.

2. Show a flashcard to a student.
3. The student makes a sentence using 'need' (e.g., 'You need to bring an umbrella.')
4. The correct sentence gets a point.

Game 2: Need Relay

Materials: Slips of paper with incomplete sentences (e.g., 'I __ go now.')How to Play:
1. Place the sentence slips at the other end of the room.
2. Students run one by one, pick a slip, run back and complete it using 'need' correctly.
3. The team that finishes all correctly first wins

More Examples and Explanations

Using 'Need' in Different Tenses and Forms

Although 'need' as a modal verb is typically used in the present, we can look at how it behaves in context:
1. You needn't go there now. (Present)
2. He said I needn't have done it. (Past meaning -it was not necessary but I did it)
3. Need they speak so loudly? (Question form)

Main Verb 'Need' -More Practice

Examples in different forms:
-Present: She needs to eat more vegetables.
-Past: They needed to finish the task by

Friday.-Negative: We don't need to call them now.

More Exercises

Exercise 4: Rewrite using 'need' correctly

1. It is not necessary for you to worry. → You __ worry.
2. Is it necessary for me to go now? → __ I go now?
3. She has to study. → She __ to study.

Exercise 5: Correct the Mistakes
1. He need to finish his work.
2. I doesn't need to help them.
3. Need she to do it?
4. You need not to come.

Game 3: Need Sentence Puzzle

Materials: Words printed on cards to form sentences.

How to Play:
1. Break the class into small groups.
2. Give each group a set of jumbled cards.
3. Students race to form correct 'need' sentences (both modal and main verb forms).

Game 4: What Do We Need?

How to Play:
1. One student acts out a situation (e.g., going to the beach).

2. Others guess and say sentences like 'You need to take sunscreen.'3. The best and most accurate sentence wins points.

Need Bingo

How to Play:

Prepare Bingo cards with different sentences using "need" (e.g., "I need to clean my room," "She doesn't need to go outside").

Read out sentences randomly to the students.

If they have the sentence on their card, they mark it off.

The first student to mark off all their sentences and shout "Bingo!" wins!

Purpose:This game helps students listen for correct use of "need" in sentences.

4. Need Charades

How to Play:

Write different activities or actions on pieces of paper (e.g., "study," "eat breakfast," "go to the gym").

One student draws a piece of paper and acts out the activity.

The other students must guess the activity and form a sentence using "need" (e.g., "I need to study").

The student who guesses correctly gets a turn

to act out the next activity.

Purpose: This game helps students practice using "need" in a fun, interactive way.

Modal Verb: MAY

An In-depth Learning Resource for English Language Students

Includes: Theory, Examples, Exercises, Vocabulary, Activities, Game, and Glossary

1. May Modal Verb: Explanation and Examples

The modal verb 'may' is primarily used to express:

1. Possibility– something that could happen or be true.
2. Permission– asking for or granting permission in a formal or polite way.
3. Wishes – often used in formal, hopeful expressions.
4. Polite Suggestions– soft recommendations or requests.

Grammar Structure:

'May' is followed by the base form of the main verb (bare infinitive).

Subject + may + verb (bare infinitive)

Examples:

- It may rain this evening. (Possibility)

- May I come in? (Permission)
- May you live long and prosper. (Wish)
- You may want to double-check your answer. (Polite suggestion)

Duration:
15–20 minutes
Materials Needed:
Pre-made "Secret Role Cards" (or slips of paper) with mysterious characters or situations
A guessing board or whiteboard (optional)
Small prizes or points system (optional)
How to Play:
1. Preparation:
Prepare role cards. Each card contains a short identity or scenario. Examples:
"You are a time traveler from the future."
"You are lost in a magical forest."
"You are an alien trying to find your spaceship."
"You are a famous singer in disguise."
Each student draws one card without showing others.
2. Game Rules:
One student comes to the front (or is in the

spotlight in their group).
They pick a card secretly and read it (without showing).
The rest of the group starts asking "May I…" questions to guess the identity or situation.
Example:
"May I ask if you are human?"
"May I ask what year you are from?"
"May I ask if you can sing?"
"May I ask if you're hiding from someone?"
The student can only answer Yes/No or respond with "You may not ask that" for mystery.

3. Winning the Round:
The first student who guesses correctly becomes the next role-player.
The game continues until each student has had a turn or time is up.

Language Focus:
Polite permission: May I ask…?
Restriction: You may not…
Possibility: You may be… / It may be…

Bonus Twists (Optional):
Give points for correct grammar and creativity.
Add a "time limit" per turn for fast-paced

action.

Include fun sound effects or role-play props to boost energy.

Learning Outcome:

Students actively use "may" in realistic and imaginative contexts, reinforcing polite forms and modal verb usage while having fun and practicing speaking skills.

2. Exercises

A. Complete the sentences using 'may':
1. She ___ call us later today.
2. ___ I open the window?
3. They ___ not agree with your opinion.

B. Rewrite using 'may':
1. Is it okay if I take a photo? → _____
2. I hope you succeed. → _____

C. Correct the mistakes:
1. He mays arrive late. → _____
2. May she to go home? → _____

10 Grammar Questions with "May"
1. May I borrow your pen for a moment?
2. What may happen if it rains tomorrow?
3. May we leave early today?
4. Why may she not attend the meeting?
5. Who may answer the question next?
6. May I open the window, please?

7. Where may he be at this time of day?
8. May students use their phones during the break?
9. What may cause the machine to stop working?
10. May I ask you a personal question?
D. Translation:
1. Balki u bugun darsga kelmas. → _____

2. Ruxsat bersangiz derazani ochsam bo'ladimi? → _____

Activity Name: "Mystery May!" – A Guessing & Speaking Game
Level: Pre-Intermediate to Intermediate
Skills Practiced: Speaking, Listening, Modal usage (Possibility & Permission)
Focus Modal: May
How to Play
1. Preparation:
Write 10 mysterious "situations" on slips of paper (or show them on screen).
Each situation should give a clue about something that may be happening or may have happened.
Examples of mystery clues:
There's water on the floor and the window is

open.
The classroom lights are off, but it's only 10 a.m.
A lunchbox is on the table, but no one is around.
There's a birthday card on the teacher's desk.
You hear music from the next room.

2. Student Roles:

One student (or pair/group) draws a "mystery."
They must explain what may be happening using "may."

Example Response:

There's water on the floor and the window is open.
"It may have rained and the wind blew the window open."
"Someone may have spilled water and left quickly."

3. The class votes on the most likely or most creative explanation using "may."

Optional Extension: "May I...?" Polite Roleplay

After the guessing round, switch gears.
Students roleplay polite requests using "may I...?" in everyday situations:

May I borrow your pencil?
May I leave the classroom early today?
May I join your team?
Language Focus / Follow-Up:
Review differences between "may" (possibility) and "may I" (permission).
Ask students to write their own mystery clue and challenge a partner.

3. Vocabulary

Useful expressions and collocations with 'may':
- May I have your attention, please?
- You may be right.
- There may be a problem with the internet.
- May I suggest an alternative?
- This may cause confusion.

Synonyms for 'may' (in certain contexts):
- Might (possibility)
- Could (possibility)
- Can (informal permission)

10 Grammar Practice Questions for "Might":

1. What might you do if you finish your homework early today?
(Practice making suggestions or possibilities in the future.)

2. Think about a mystery movie — what might happen next in the story?

(Practice using "might" for predicting possible events.)
3.Your friend looks upset. What might be the reason?
(Practice expressing guesses and possibilities.)
4.Imagine you see a dark cloud in the sky. What might that mean?
(Practice describing possible weather changes.)
5.You lost your phone. Where might you have left it?
(Practice "might have + past participle" for past possibility.)
6.What might happen if people stop using plastic bags?
(Practice using "might" for hypothetical situations and consequences.)
7.You hear a strange noise in the kitchen. What might be causing it?
(Practice using "might" to express uncertain causes.)
8.What might someone say if they want to ask for permission politely?
(Link to modal "may" and understand polite forms.)
9.Describe a future technology that might exist in 2050.

(Practice creative future possibilities with "might".)
10. If you had more free time, what hobbies might you try?
(Practice using "might" in second conditional-like sentences.)

QUESTIONS:
 A. MUST (strong obligation or necessity)
1. What must students do to succeed in school?
2. Must we bring our books to every class?
3. What must people do to stay healthy?
4. Must you wear a uniform at your workplace?
5. What must tourists know before visiting your country?
B. HAVE TO (obligation or necessity)
6. Do you have to do chores at home?
7. What time do you have to get up on weekdays?
8. Does your teacher have to check homework every day?
9. What do people have to do before taking an exam?
10. Did you have to study last weekend?
 C. CAN (ability or permission)

11. What can you cook by yourself?
12. Can students use dictionaries during tests?
13. Where can we find good English books?
14. What sports can you play well?
15. Can you travel alone at your age?

10 Grammar Test Questions with "May"

1. Multiple Choice

___ I ask you a personal question?

a) Must
b) Can
c) May
d) Have to

2. Fill in the Blank

It's cloudy today. It ___ rain later, so take an umbrella.

3. Error Correction

Find and correct the error:

You may to leave now if you're finished

4. Sentence Transformation

Rewrite the sentence using "may" to make it more polite:

Can I join your group?

→ ___

5. Multiple Choice

Which sentence expresses possibility?

a) You may take a seat.

b) I may visit London this summer.
c) May I speak now?
d) May you carry my bag?

6. Fill in the Blank

You ___ not use your phone during the exam.

7. Sentence Completion

Complete the sentence:

They're not sure, but she ___ be at home by now.

8. Multiple Choice

Choose the correct sentence:

a) I may going to the market.
b) He may goes to school.
c) We may go hiking tomorrow.
d) May she to call now?

9. Correct the Mistake

Find and fix the error:

May he to borrow your dictionary?

10. Fill in the Blank

Students ___ enter the library only with a teacher's permission.

4. Activity

Group Activity: 'Permission and Possibility Dialogue'

Objective: Practice using 'may' in context.

Instructions:

1. Form pairs or small groups.
2. One student acts as a teacher, boss, or parent; the other as a student, employee, or child.
3. Create a short dialogue using 'may' to ask permission and express possibility.
Example Dialogue:
- Student: May I submit the assignment tomorrow?
- Teacher: Yes, you may, but it may be marked late.

10 Grammar Questions on "Need"
1. Write a sentence using "need to" to talk about daily routine.
2. Make a question with "need to" about school.
3. Write a sentence using "don't need to" to express something unnecessary.
4. Change this sentence to the negative form: She needs to clean the room.
5. Use "needn't" in a sentence to show that something is not necessary.
6. Make a sentence with "need" as a main verb in the present simple.
7. Make a question with "Does she need".
8. Rewrite this sentence using "needn't":

You don't need to wear a uniform.
9. Write a sentence with "needed to" in the past.
10. Write a question with "Did you need to".
5. Game
Game: 'Modal Maze'
Objective: Reinforce understanding of when and how to use 'may'.
Instructions:
1. Create a 'maze' of sentences on cards—some correct, some incorrect.
2. Students pick a path by choosing cards with correctly used 'may' forms.
3. Incorrect choices lead to a 'dead end'.
4. First to reach the end wins.
Sample Correct:
- May I leave early today?
- It may take some time.
Sample Incorrect:
- She mays go now.
- May to I come in?
Vocabulary for "Must"
Must means something is very important or necessary.
You use it when there is no choice.
Useful words to learn with "must":

Obliged – You have to do it because it's the rule or law.
(e.g., You are obliged to wear a seatbelt.)
Mandatory – Something that is required.
(e.g., Wearing a uniform is mandatory at this school.)
Prohibited – Not allowed at all.
(e.g., Phones are prohibited in the exam room.)
Essential – Very important.
(e.g., It is essential to get enough sleep.)
Urgent – Needs to be done very quickly.
(e.g., You must call the doctor. It's urgent.)
 Vocabulary for "Have to"
Have to is used when someone else or a situation says it is necessary.
It's often about rules, duties, or routines.
Useful words to learn with "have to":
Required – You need to do it.
(e.g., You are required to do homework.)
Deadline – A time limit to finish something.
(e.g., I have to finish the project by Friday.)
Responsibility – Something you must take care of.
(e.g., Parents have to take responsibility for their children.)
Routine – Something you do every day.

(e.g., I have to brush my teeth in the morning.)
Duty – A job or task you must do
(e.g., Soldiers have to do their duty.)
Vocabulary for "Can"
Can is used to show ability, permission, or possibility.
Useful words to learn with "can":
Ability – What someone is able to do.
(e.g., She can play the piano.)
Possibility – Something that might happen.
(e.g., It can rain in the evening.)
Permission – Being allowed to do something.
(e.g., You can leave now.)
Opportunity – A chance to do something.
(e.g., You can join the club if you like.)
Skill – Something you are good at doing.
(e.g., He can draw very well.)
Role Play Activity: "Mystery at the International Airport"
 Objective:
To help students practice using "might" to express possibility and uncertainty in a real-world situation through role play.
 Participants:
4–8 students per group (adaptable to class size)
 Time:

20–30 minutes

Scenario:

A suspicious suitcase is found unattended in an international airport terminal. The airport security team must interview nearby passengers and make decisions about what the suitcase might contain and who might have left it.

Roles:

Assign each student a role (or let them choose):
1. Airport Security Officer (1–2 students)
2. Tourist from France
3. Businessperson from Japan
4. Student from Brazil
5. Family from Egypt (1 or 2 students)
6. Suspicious Person (secretly assigned)

Each character has a unique alibi or story. For example:

The tourist might have gone to buy a coffee.

The businessperson might have confused the suitcase with theirs.

The student might be looking for their charger.

The suspicious person might be nervous and hiding something.

Instructions:
1. Set the scene:

"An unidentified suitcase is found near Gate 7. Security must investigate who it might belong to, and what it might contain. The passengers nearby are being questioned."

2. Preparation (5–10 mins):

Students create short background stories for their roles.

Each character must think of 2–3 things they might say or suggest using the modal "might".

(e.g., "It might belong to the person who just left." / "It might be a gift from my friend.")

3. Role Play (10–15 mins):

The security officers ask questions:

"Where were you 10 minutes ago?"

"Do you know what this suitcase might contain?"

Each character responds in character using "might" to explain, suggest, or deny.

The security officers try to figure out the most likely owner or determine if it's a threat.

4. Wrap-up Discussion (5 mins):

Who was the most suspicious?

What might really have been in the suitcase?

What language did students use to express uncertainty?

Language Focus:

Might for possibility:
"It might be someone else's."
"I might have seen that bag before."
Might have + past participle:
"He might have left it by accident."
 Assessment / Feedback:
Award "Best Role Performance" or "Best Use of 'Might'"
Encourage peer feedback: "Which student used 'might' most naturally?"
 Vocabulary for "May"
May is used for formal or polite permission and possibility.
Useful words to learn with "may":
Polite request – Asking nicely.
(e.g., May I use your phone?)
Possibility – Something that might happen.
(e.g., It may snow tomorrow.)
Uncertainty – When you're not sure.
(e.g., She may come to the party.)
Permission – Formal way to say "You are allowed".
(e.g., Students may leave after class.)
Formal tone – Used when you want to sound polite or respectful.
(e.g., May I introduce my friend?)

10 Grammar Questions with "Need"
1. What do you need to take to school every day?
2. Does she need any help with her homework?
3. Do we need to bring our books tomorrow?
4. Why do they need to study so hard?
5. Who needs to finish the project today?
6. Did you need to go to the doctor last week?
7. What did he need to buy at the store?
8. Why don't you need to clean your room today?
9. Need I finish it now, or can I do it later?
10. What do we need to do before the test?

6. Glossary

- Modal Verb: A helping verb that adds meaning to the main verb (e.g., may, can, must).
- Possibility: A chance that something may happen.
- Permission: Consent to do something.
- Politeness: Respectful or considerate language use.
- Bare Infinitive: The base form of a verb without 'to'.

- **Suggestion:** An idea or plan put forward for consideration.
- **Formal Language:** Language used in serious or official communication.
- **Dialogue:** A conversation between two or more people.

TABLE OF CONTENTS

Introduction
CHAPTER I: Understanding Modal Verbs
1.1. "Should" – Definition, Usage and Examples
1.2. "Would" – Definition, Usage and Examples
1.3. "Should" and "Would" – Comparison and Application Cases
CHAPTER II: Practice Exercises ('Should' and 'Would')
2.1. Fill in the blanks
2.2. Determine whether it is true or false
2.3. Rewrite the sentences (with 'should'/'would')
2.4. Exercises with translations and questions
2.5. Written assignment
CHAPTER III: Modal Verbs 'Can', 'Must' and 'Have to'
3.1. 'Can' – Ability, Permission, Possibility and Requests
3.2. 'Must' – Strong Obligations and Rules
3.3. 'Have to' / 'Has to' – External obligation
3.4. Comparative analysis and examples
3.5. Exercises and tests

CHAPTER IV: The modal verb 'Need'
4.1. 'Need' – as a Modal and Main Verb
4.2. Examples with rules and structures
4.3. Exercises
CHAPTER V: The modal verb 'May'
5.1. 'May' – Possibility, Permission, Desire and Recommendation
5.2. Games, activities, exercises
5.3. Exercises and translations
CHAPTER VI: 'Might' – a modal indicating probability
6.1. 'Might' – Examples, Exercises, Games
CHAPTER VII: Games and Practical Activities
7.1. Role-playing games, group work
7.2. Reinforcement through interactive exercises
CHAPTER VIII: Glossary (Dictionary)
8.1. Modal Verb Words and Phrases
8.2. Thematic Dictionary
CHAPTER IX: Written and Oral Practices
9.1. Written Exercises - Tips and Ideas
9.2. Writing and Constructing Dialogues
9.3. Oral Expression Exercises
CHAPTER X: Tests Section
10.1. 'Must', 'Have to', 'Can' Tests

10.2. 'Need', 'May', 'Might' Tests
10.3. Mixed Tests and General Questions
CHAPTER XI: Final Exercises and Review
11.1. Comparing Modal Verbs, Tests
11.2. Paragraph Writing and Assessment Criteria
Concluding Remarks

MUNDARIJA

Kirish
I BOB: Modal Fe'llarning Tushunchasi
1.1. "Should" – Ta'rifi, Qo'llanilishi va Misollar
1.2. "Would" – Ta'rifi, Qo'llanilishi va Misollar
1.3. "Should" va "Would" – Taqqoslash va Qo'llash Holatlari
II BOB: Amaliy Mashqlar ('Should' va 'Would')
2.1. Bo'sh joylarni to'ldiring
2.2. To'g'ri yoki noto'g'riligini aniqlang
2.3. Gaplarni qayta yozing ('should'/'would' bilan)
2.4. Tarjimalar va savollar bilan mashqlar
2.5. Yozma topshiriq
III BOB: 'Can', 'Must' va 'Have to' modal fe'llari
3.1. 'Can' – Qobiliyat, Ruxsat, Imkoniyat va So'rovlar
3.2. 'Must' – Kuchli majburiyat va Qoidalar
3.3. 'Have to' / 'Has to' – Tashqi majburiyat
3.4. Taqqosiy tahlil va misollar
3.5. Mashqlar va testlar
IV BOB: 'Need' modal fe'li
4.1. 'Need' – Modal va Asosiy fe'l sifatida
4.2. Qoida va strukturalar bilan misollar
4.3. Mashqlar
V BOB: 'May' modal fe'li
5.1. 'May' – Imkoniyat, Ruxsat, Istak va Tavsiya
5.2. O'yinlar, faoliyatlar, mashqlar
5.3. Mashqlar va tarjimalar
VI BOB: 'Might' – ehtimollik bildiruvchi modal

6.1. 'Might' – Misollar, Mashqlar, O'yinlar
VII BOB: O'yinlar va Amaliy Faoliyatlar
7.1. Rolli o'yinlar, guruhli ishlash
7.2. Interaktiv mashqlar orqali mustahkamlash
VIII BOB: Glossary (Lug'at)
8.1. Modal fe'llarga oid so'z va iboralar
8.2. Tematik lug'at
IX BOB: Yozma va Og'zaki Amaliyotlar
9.1. Yozma mashq – maslahatlar va tasavvurlar
9.2. Dialog yozish va tuzish
9.3. Og'zaki ifoda mashqlari
X BOB: Testlar Bo'limi
10.1. 'Must', 'Have to', 'Can' testlari
10.2. 'Need', 'May', 'Might' testlari
10.3. Aralash testlar va umumiy savollar
XI BOB: Yakuniy Mashqlar va Takrorlash
11.1. Modal fe'llarni qiyoslash, testlar
11.2. Paragraf yozish va baholash mezonlari
Tugatish so'zi

Allaberganova Umida Maqsud qizi was born on September 1, 2005 in Bagat district of Khorezm region. 2nd year student of Foreign Philology and Literature at Urgench State Pedagogical Institute. She is the owner of C1 in IELTS with 7 band score and also works in Humo language centre as a teacher.

During her studies, she has published 12 articles related to English language teaching and literature in both international and republic journals. For example, her first article titled "Enriching the spiritual world of children through samples of folklore" was published in "Eurasian Journal of Social Sciences, Philosophy and Culture" in 24.01.2024. This article explores how article can shape children's moral and cultural development, reflecting her deep interest in literature as an educational tool. Furthermore, her second article is called "Effectiveness of reading English literature while preparing for IELTS" which was presented in republic conference.

Moreover, she has published two books: one titled "The role of literature in learning foreign languages" and the other "Learning English Grammar".

Furthermore, she has been selected as a Finalist for 2025 Leaders of Tomorrow Exchange Program (LOT).

Umida Allaberganova, a student of the English Language and Literature at Urgench State Pedagogical Institute, successfully participated in the international publicistic works competition titled "Живые образы" (Living Images), held in Russia from June 1 to 15, 2024.

In this competition, Umida Allaberganova

achieved outstanding results thanks to her solid knowledge, creative abilities, and scientific research skills.

She participated with her creative work titled "Stixotvorenie" (Poem), which was highly praised and awarded the First-Degree Winner's Diploma in the nomination "Artistic Word among University and College Students".

In addition, she actively participated in "Registon IELTS granti" and was awarded with a certificate after taking high scores.

www.ingramcontent.com/pod-product-compliance
Lightning Source LLC
LaVergne TN
LVHW021230080526
838199LV00089B/5984